The Piccolo Puppet Book

The Piccolo
Puppet Book

Delphine Evans

cover and text illustrations by Juliet Stanwell-Smith

Piccolo Original Pan Books

Contents

First published 1977 by Pan Books Ltd,
Cavaye Place, London sw10 9pg
2nd printing 1977
© Delphine Evans 1977
ISBN 0 330 25040 X
Filmset in 'Monophoto' Baskerville 12 on 13 pt and
printed in Great Britain by
Richard Clay (The Chaucer Press) Ltd, Bungay, Suffolk

Introduction

In this book you will find puppets of all shapes and sizes for you to make.

Some are made from odds and ends, some are from new materials. Some you sew, some you glue together. Some are easy, some are hard to make.

All are fun!

If you intend making quite a few puppets, it's a good idea to start a *bitbox*.

You need a box with a lid – like a chocolate box. Inside it keep things which will be useful for the puppets' features and decoration, like sequins, small buttons, beads and small plastic things (for features); fur, wool, string and feathers (for hair and whiskers); short 'bits' of lace and ribbon and small 'bits' of felt, material, coloured paper and foil (for decoration).

Quality is more important than quantity.

If you also keep your scissors, needle, cotton, felt-tip pens and glue in the box, you will be ready to start just whenever you want to!

Note It is important to use the correct type of glue – particularly when sticking plastic and polystyrene – so, read the label carefully to avoid disappointing results.

Bells, joggle eyes, polystyrene balls, etc, can be bought in most craft or hobby shops.

1 Matchbox puppets

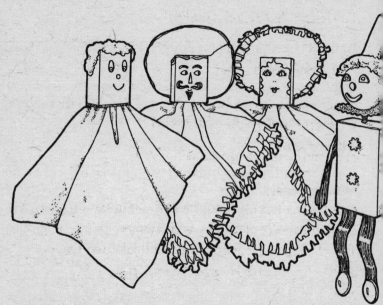

Mickey Hankey, Tish and Ooo, Wobble Clown

To help you make the puppets in this chapter, your *bitbox* should have the following things in it:
empty matchboxes, tissues, cotton wool, plain paper, buttons, ribbon, sequins, felt, fur fabric, felt-tip pens, glue and scissors.

Mickey Hankey

You will need

1 matchbox cover
a small amount of cotton wool
1 paper tissue
glue and felt-tip pens

What you do

Draw a face on the plain side of your matchbox cover.

Arrange cotton wool in the top for hair, and glue this into place.

Drape tissue over your hand and slide the matchbox cover over the first two fingers.

Say 'hello' to Mickey Hankey!

Tish and Ooo

You will need

2 matchboxes
6 coloured tissues (3 of each colour)
a piece of plain paper
glue, felt-tip pens and scissors

What you do

Cover the matchbox covers with plain paper.

Cut two circles of paper 10cm across.

Cover each circle with a different coloured tissue.

Place the matchbox cover on end in the centre and draw round its outline.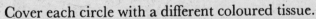

Cut round the outline and fit it over the top of the matchbox cover for the hat.

For Ooo's hat
Make 1cm cuts round the edge and stick the sides of the hat to the sides of the box, to make a bonnet.

Draw on the faces.

Place two tissues together and fold them
in half to make a
triangle.

Make 1cm cuts
round the edges
for frills.

Cut a small hole in the centre.
Gather this middle portion together and glue it inside the
bottom of your matchbox. Now Tish and Ooo are ready
to use.

Wobble Clown

You will need
1 matchbox
1 polystyrene or ping-pong ball
4 strips of ribbon about 5cm long
4 buttons
1 small spring
glue
oddments of felt, fur fabric and sequins

What you do
Take the 'drawer' from the matchbox and cut off one
short side.

Slide it back into place.

Cover the matchbox with felt
(leaving the cut side of the
drawer open).

Cut out a nose 𝑂 and a mouth ⌣ from the felt.

Using sequins for eyes, glue the features into place on the
ball.

Find a small piece of fur fabric
and glue this onto the ball
for hair.

Hat

Using the felt, cut a triangle shape 4cm × 4cm.

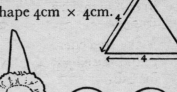

Glue the long sides together.

Glue it into place on the clown's head.

Ruff

Cut a circle of felt 4cm across.

Cut a small hole in the centre of it to make a ruff.

Glue it onto the neck end of the head.

Assembly

Make a hole in the top of the matchbox and in the neck end of the ball (to fit the spring).

Insert the spring into both holes to make a wobbly neck.

Glue a button onto one end of each ribbon and glue the other end of the ribbons onto the front of the matchbox for arms and legs.

Insert two fingers inside the box and make him dance. Sit him on a shelf and watch his legs dangle and his head 'wobble'.

2 Cheesebox puppets

Mr Round, Happy/Sad Puppet

To help you make the puppets in this chapter, your *bitbox*
should have the following things in it:
round cheese boxes, pipe cleaners, matchbox, oddments of
felt, fur fabric and material, needle, cotton and scissors,
felt-tip pens and glue.

Mr Round

You will need

1 round cheesebox
2 pipe cleaners
oddments of material and felt
glue, felt-tip pens and scissors

What you do

Cut a half circle of pink felt, 1cm larger than the cheesebox.

Cut a half circle of another colour, 1cm larger than the cheesebox.

Glue these onto the outside cover of the cheesebox.
Glue the overlap down round the edges.

Cut two eyes from the blue felt ◉ ◉ a red nose △ and a mouth. ◡

Glue these into place on the pink half of the cheesebox.

Using different coloured felts, cut out a hat ⌐_⌐ and a hat-band ▬ and a belt.

Glue these into place, as shown.

To make the arms
Bend the pipe cleaners in half and thread them through the sides of the box. Cut two small pieces of pink felt for the hands ⊂⟩ ⟨⊃ and glue them into place on the ends of the pipe cleaners.

Cut two round holes in the bottom part of the box to put your fingers through for Mr Round's legs.

Happy/Sad Puppet

You will need

1 round cheesebox, with lid
2 pieces of material 15cm × 25cm
1 matchbox cover
strands of wool or a strip of fur fabric (for hair)
oddments of felt
glue and scissors

What you do

Cut a hole in the rims of the
cheesebox and lid to fit over the matchbox.
Glue the matchbox cover into place inside
the cheesebox, as shown.

Glue the lid of the cheesebox to the other side of the
matchbox cover and fix the edges of the cheesebox and lid
together with adhesive tape round the outside.

Cut out two sets of features from the felt,
one happy and one sad.

Glue them into place on either side of the box.

Glue a narrow strip of fur fabric (or strands
of wool) onto the top edge of the box for hair.
Put the two pieces of material on top of
each other and cut out a dress shape for
the body of the puppet.

Glue the two dress shapes together
along the edges,
leaving the neck and bottom edge open.

Ease it onto the matchbox and glue it into position.
Cut out two felt hands and two bow ties.

Glue them into place on both sides of the puppet.

Put him on your hand and
see him look happy or sad!

3 Mitten, sock and glove puppets

Kitten Mitten, Funny Face, Walrus, Polly

To help you make the puppets in this chapter your *bitbox* should have the following things in it:
old mittens, gloves and socks, buttons, ribbon, felt and material, fur fabric, wool, glue and felt-tip pens, needle and cotton.

Kitten Mitten

You will need

1 old fur mitten   wool
oddments of felt   glue
a length of ribbon

What you do

Using different coloured felts, cut out two sets of circles for eyes,  and a nose.

Cut three strands of wool for whiskers.

Glue them all into place on the palm side of the mitten, as shown.

Cut out two felt ears and glue them into place at the top end of the mitten.

Tie a bow of ribbon round his neck and you have a 'kitten from a mitten'.

Funny Face

You will need

1 old mitten
oddments of felt
2 joggle eyes, if you can get them

What you do

Using the felt, cut out two circles for eyes (or use the joggle eyes), a triangle nose and two lips.

Holding the mitten sideways, glue them into place, as shown, making sure the lips are in the correct position.

Put on the mitten and make Funny Face talk – by moving your thumb.

Walrus

You will need

1 old sock
2 bright buttons
1 dull button

white fur fabric or wool
glue
needle and cotton

What you do

Sew or glue the dull button in the middle at the end of the sock.

To make a moustache, glue some short pieces of white wool or fur fabric to either side of the button.

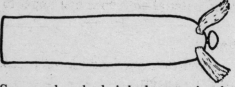

Sew or glue the bright buttons in place for eyes.

Slip him over your hand and Walrus is ready to use.

Polly

You will need

1 old glove (a thin one if possible)
1 polystyrene ball, or similar
a piece of material approximately 25cm × 13cm
a piece of material cut into a triangle to fit the ball
oddments of fur fabric
2 sequins
glue and felt-tip pen

What you do

Make a hole in the polystyrene ball, large enough to fit your first finger.

Glue the sequins onto the ball for eyes.

Using a felt-tip pen, draw on a nose and a mouth.

18

Glue a strip of fur fabric round the face for hair.

Tie or glue the triangle piece of material round it for a scarf.

Cut a hole in the centre of the larger piece of material.

Assembly

Put the glove on your hand.

Slide the large piece of material onto your first finger to make a shawl.

Place the head on top.

Curl up your third and fourth fingers and use your second finger and thumb for Polly's arms.

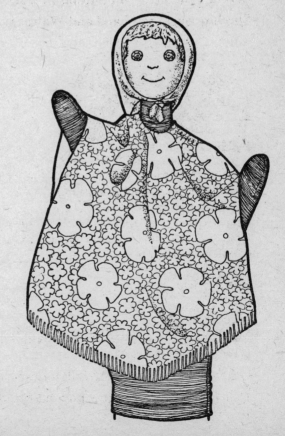

4 Mop and spoon puppets

Sally Spoon, Wendy Wooden Spoon, Milly Mop

To help you make the puppets in this chapter your *bitbox*
should have the following things in it:
old spoons (plastic, wooden or metal), spatulas, pipe
cleaners, paper cake cases, material, felt, paper, wool and
ribbon, glue, felt-tip pens and scissors, needle and cotton.

Sally Spoon

You will need
1 old teaspoon or spatula
1 paper cake case
a piece of material approximately 10cm × 15cm
oddments of paper or felt (for features)
wool (for hair)
glue
scissors

What you do
Using the felt cut out two eyes ◯ ◯ a nose △ and
a mouth. ◠

Glue these into position on the back of the spoon.

Glue the two short edges
of the material together.

Gather the top of the material together and glue it to the spoon just below the bowl.

To make Sally's hair
Cut the wool into strands, long enough to fit over the top of her head and hang down to her 'shoulders'.

Place the paper cake case round the edge of the bowl to make a bonnet.

Glue it into place.

Make Sally more attractive by putting a bow in her hair.

Wendy Wooden Spoon

You will need
1 wooden spoon
2 pipe cleaners
material: 1 piece 18cm × 38cm and a long strip
   about 10cm wide
oddments of wool and felt
glue
needle, cotton and scissors

What you do
Cut out two eyes o o
a nose △
and a mouth. ⌣
Glue them into place on the back of the spoon.

To make Wendy's hair
Cut the wool into strands about 30cm long and glue it round the face.

Twist the two pipe cleaners together 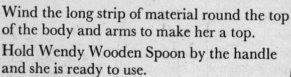 and glue them to the handle for arms.

Glue or sew the two short sides of the material together.

Using long stitches, gather it along the top edge and glue it to the body just below the arms.

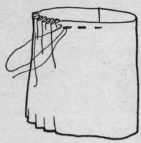

Wind the long strip of material round the top of the body and arms to make her a top.

Hold Wendy Wooden Spoon by the handle and she is ready to use.

Milly Mop

You will need
1 dish mop
1 powder puff, or a circle of foam
6cm across
2 pipe cleaners
1 piece of material 18cm × 38cm
glue
felt-tip pens
needle, cotton and scissors

What you do

Using a felt-tip pen, draw a face
on the powder puff.

Glue the puff
onto the mop handle.

Twist the pipe cleaners together
and glue them into place
for arms.

Glue or sew the two short sides
of the material together and,
using long stitches, gather it
along the top to make
the skirt.

Glue the skirt onto the mop handle,
just below the arms.

To make Milly Mop more
attractive, glue a bow of
ribbon in her hair.

5 Cardboard puppets

Trumper Cut-out, Swimming Fishes

To help you make the puppets in this chapter your *bitbox* should have the following things in it:
plain postcards, silver foil and sequins, tracing paper, a pencil and felt-tip pens, scissors and cotton.

Trumper Cut-out

You will need
1 postcard
tracing paper
pencil and
felt-tip pens
scissors

What you do
Trace this drawing and transfer it to your postcard.

Now colour it.
Trumper's colours are:
ears – pink
eyes – white outside, then pink, then black
fur – dark grey
jumper – green
dungarees   black and white check

Cut round the outline, making a hole where the trunk
should be.
Now make your finger into the trunk by putting it
through the hole, and wriggle it – as Trumper does!

Swimming Fishes

You will need
silver foil
cardboard
sewing cotton
sequins (for eyes)
scissors, pencil and glue

What you do
Copy the shape of the fish onto
the cardboard, and cut it out.

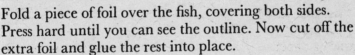

Fold a piece of foil over the fish, covering both sides.
Press hard until you can see the outline. Now cut off the
extra foil and glue the rest into place.

Glue on the eyes and any other decoration you like.

Thread the fish
with cotton.

Make several fishes and thread them with cotton of
different lengths.
Hang them on a pencil and see them swim!
An idea on how to use them is on page 92.

6 Ball puppets

Spider and Octopus, Frog, Bluey, Charlie Clown, Bird

To help you make the puppets in this chapter, your *bitbox* should have the following things in it:
paper and cardboard, pipe cleaners, thin elastic, milk bottle tops, washing-up liquid bottle tops, feathers, foil, ribbon, felt and fur fabric oddments, sequins, needle and cotton, scissors and glue.

Spider and Octopus

You will need

polystyrene, ping-pong or cotton ball
4 pipe cleaners (orange or black)
orange or black enamel paint (the sort used for painting plastic
  models)
oddments of coloured paper and cardboard
a length of thin elastic
the small plastic cap from a washing-up   foil
liquid bottle (for Octopus)   scissors
a milk bottle top (for Spider)   glue

What you do

Make eight small holes in the ball
in the position of legs.

Paint the ball – orange for Octopus or black for Spider.

When the ball is dry, cut the pipe cleaners in half and
push them into the holes.
Curl them to look like legs.

For Octopus

Make a hole in the plastic cap of a washing-up liquid
bottle and thread a short length of elastic through.

Cut a small round of cardboard and glue
the cap to it, to make the hat.

Glue the hat to the ball.

Cut out paper eyes, a nose
and a mouth and glue them
into place.

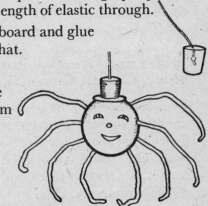

For Spider

Using your finger, bend a milk bottle top into a hat shape.

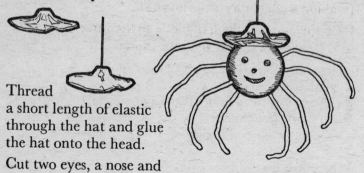

Thread a short length of elastic through the hat and glue the hat onto the head.

Cut two eyes, a nose and a mouth out of silver foil and glue them into place.

Frog

You will need

a hollow rubber or plastic ball, about 10cm across, orange, brown or green
a sheet of green foam 45cm × 20cm
oddments of orange and yellow felt
joggle eyes
scissors, tracing paper and pencil
glue

What you do

Ask a grown-up to cut the ball in half.

Cut out a circle of foam, the same measurement across as the ball.

Cut a half-circle of foam the same size as half the ball, and slice out a piece, as shown.

Cut an oval of foam. To do this, make the ends the same size as the circle of foam but extend the middle about 2½cm.

Glue the ordinary circle round the cut edge of the ball.

Fold the oval in half and glue its top edge to the circle (making a pocket for your fingers).

Glue the curve of the half-circle to the underside of the oval (making a pocket for your thumb).

Cut out a felt tongue and a nose.

Glue them into place.

Trace the patterns for the eyes.

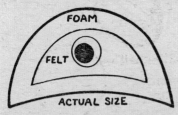

Cut them out and make the eyes as follows: foam outside – felt next – then the joggles.

Glue them into place on top of the ball.

Trace the pattern on the next page for the legs.

Cut two legs of foam and glue them to the underside of the body.

Frog is now ready to use.

Bluey

You will need

a hollow blue rubber or plastic ball, about 10cm across
a sheet of blue foam 38cm × 20cm
plastic eyes and nose (from a hobby shop)
oddments of felt, ribbon and white foam
glue, tracing paper and pencil

What you do

Ask a grown-up to cut the ball in half.

Cut out a circle of foam the same measurement across as
the ball.

Cut out a half-circle of foam the same size as half the ball,
and slice out a piece, as shown.

Cut an oval of foam. To do this,
make the ends the same size as
the circle of foam but extend
the middle about 2½cm.

Glue the ordinary circle round the cut edge of the ball.

Fold the oval in half and glue its top edge to the circle
(making a pocket for your fingers).

Glue the curve of the half-circle to the underside of the
oval (making a pocket for your thumb).

Trace the pattern
for the ears.

Cut out two foam ears
and a felt tongue.

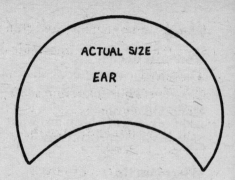

ACTUAL SIZE

EAR

Glue the ears onto the top of the ball and attach the eyes
and nose.

Trace the body shape pattern
and cut out two pieces of foam.

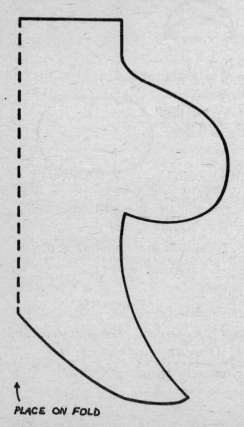

PLACE ON FOLD

Glue the sides together and stuff them if you like.

Glue the body to the underside of the head.

To complete
Cut some white foam into strips,
using pinking shears.

Glue them inside the mouth,
to look like teeth.

Make a pretty colour bow
and glue it to Bluey's neck.
Now he is ready to use.

Charlie Clown

You will need
1 polystyrene ball
2 pieces of material 18cm × 13cm
a piece of cardboard 5cm × 2·5cm
2 sequins
oddments of felt, fur fabric and foam
Needle, cotton, scissors and glue

What you do
From the felt, cut out a mouth and a nose.
Glue them into place on the ball.
Glue the two sequins on for eyes.
Cut a strip of fur fabric and glue it
onto the top of the ball, for hair.
Glue the two short sides of the
cardboard piece together to
make a tube to fit your first finger.
Spread some glue onto one edge and press it onto the ball
to make a neck. Hold it firm until it has stuck.

From the felt cut a circle 4cm across, for the ruff.

Cut a hole in the centre and slide it onto the neck.

Hat

Cut a circle of felt about 2·5cm across.

Cut a strip of felt 1·5cm wide and 11cm long, to fit round the edge of the circle.

Glue the two short edges together ← to make a tube.

Glue the circle to the top of the tube and glue the bottom of the tube to Charlie's head.

Body

Place the two pieces of material together and cut to a dress shape, as shown.

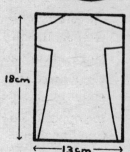

18cm

13cm

Sew or glue the sides together – leaving the neck and bottom open.

Hem the bottom edge. Gather the neck opening to fit the neck and glue it below the ruff.

Cut two hands from the felt and glue them into position.

Now Charlie is ready to use.

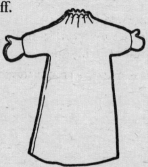

Bird

You will need
1 polystyrene ball
1 square of material 30cm × 30cm
1 piece of cardboard 2·5cm × 5cm
oddments of felt
2 sequins and a few feathers
scissors
glue (be careful to make sure it is the correct sort)

What you do

Head
First make a tube for your first finger by gluing the two short sides of the cardboard together.

Spread the glue onto one edge and press it onto the ball, to make the bird's neck.

Hold it firm until it has stuck.

Cut a piece of felt to cover the neck, and glue it into place.

Glue the eyes in position on the opposite side of the ball from the tube.

Cut a piece of felt 4cm square and glue two sides together, to make a beak.

Glue the beak into place below the eyes.

Wings and body
Fold the material in half to make a triangle.

Cut it into the shape shown.

fold

Cut 1cm slits along the open edges and make a small opening in the middle of the fold for the neck.

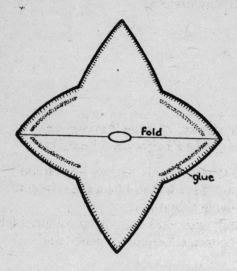

Glue the wings together (edges only – just inside the slits).

Glue the wings to the bottom part of the neck and decorate with sequins and feathers.

Insert your hand – first finger in the neck, thumb in one wing and three fingers in the other. See Bird fly!

7 Trumper and Mr Fingle

(as seen in Airfix Craft Kits, Series 5)

Trumper Hand Puppet, Mitten Trumper Walking Trumper, Mr Fingle and Family

Quite a few of the materials in this chapter need to be bought, although your *bitbox* will still be a great help to you if it has the following things in it:
sequins, a small spring, oddments of assorted coloured felt, scissors, needle and cotton, felt-tip pens, pencil and tracing paper, glue.

Trumper Hand Puppet

(as seen in Airfix Craft Kits, Series 5)

You will need

2 pieces of gingham material 15cm × 13cm
1 piece of grey foam 20cm × 13cm
1 square of grey felt 13cm × 13cm
a small amount of pink, white and green felt
pink joggle eyes
a small amount of stuffing (for Trumper's body)
needle, cotton and scissors
tracing paper and pencil
glue

What you do

Trace the patterns on pages 38 and 39. Match them to the materials stated. Pin them in place and cut them out.

With the right sides together (that is, the sides of the material you want to show when the puppet is finished),

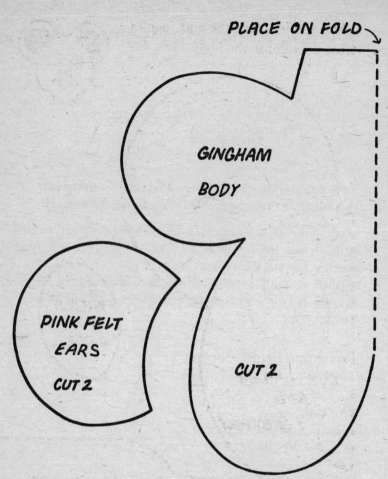

PLACE ON FOLD

GINGHAM

BODY

PINK FELT

EARS

CUT 2

CUT 2

sew or glue the two gingham pieces together – leaving the neck open.

Turn the right way out, and stuff.

Taking the grey foam for the head, glue the pink ears to it.

Glue the eyes in place –

white felt first, then the pink joggles.
Glue the head to the body.

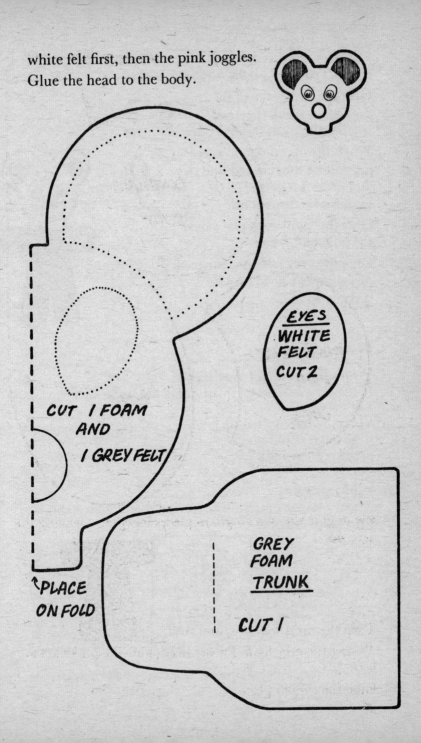

EYES
WHITE
FELT
CUT 2

CUT 1 FOAM
AND
1 GREY FELT

GREY
FOAM
TRUNK

CUT 1

↳PLACE
ON FOLD

Cut out a strip of green felt 15cm × 1cm and glue it round Trumper's neck, to make a scarf.

Glue the two edges of the grey foam trunk together, leaving the straight edge open.

When firmly stuck, put some glue along the marked line and press it together – to make the trunk curl.

Glue the trunk into place over the hole on his face.

Glue the grey felt onto the back of Trumper's head and he is ready to use.

Mitten Trumper

You will need (for one pair)
Fluorescent or reflective plastic material, approximately 45cm × 30cm
a black waterproof felt-tip pen
tracing paper and pencil
needle, cotton and glue

What you do
Make a paper pattern by drawing round your hand – fingers spread out.

Cut out the paper shape and place it on the plastic material.

Cut out four shapes from the plastic material, making sure you don't end up with four left (or right) hand-shapes.

Glue or sew two of the shapes together along the edges, leaving the straight bottom edge open.

Do the same to the other two shapes.

Trace or draw Trumper onto each mitten, so that your thumb is his trunk.

Outline Trumper with a waterproof felt-tip pen.

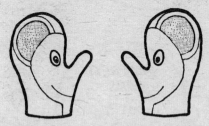

Wear your waterproof mittens whenever it rains or snows.

Walking Trumper

You will need
1 polystyrene ball
2 pieces of gingham 10cm × 10cm
oddments of grey foam, pink felt and other coloured felts
2 sequins
1 small spring
needle and cotton
grey enamel paint (the sort used for painting plastic models)
tracing paper and pencil
glue

What you do
Make a hole in the polystyrene ball, and paint it grey.

Trace the patterns on the next page and match them to the materials stated.

Pin them in place and cut them out.

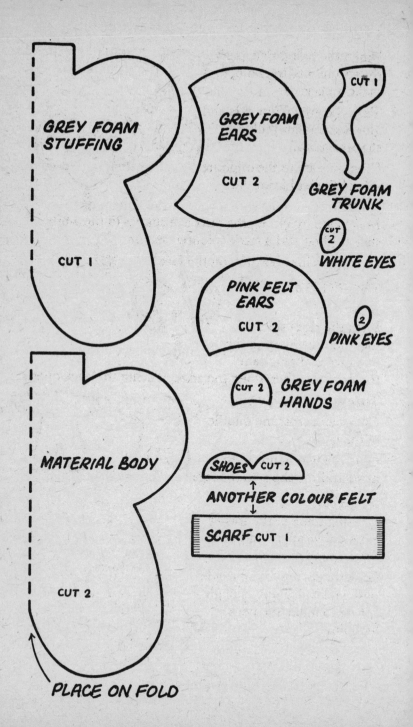

When the ball is dry, push the spring into the hole, to make a neck.

Take the grey foam ears and glue the smaller pink ear-shapes on top.

Glue the ears to the opposite side of the ball from the spring.

Make eyes by gluing the pink eye-shapes to the white shapes, then add a dark-coloured sequin.

Glue them into position on the face.

Glue on the grey trunk.

Body

With the right sides together, sew or glue the two pieces of gingham material together along the edge, leaving the neck open.

Turn the right way out.

Cut open across the middle of the back.

Glue the two hands to the arms and the shoes to the legs.

To complete

Leaving some of the spring exposed, wrap an odd piece of foam round the end.

Glue the spring to the inside of the neck, leaving enough spring to make the neck wobble.

Glue the scarf to the ball just below the trunk, so that it doesn't touch the spring.

Place the foam body inside the material body. Add a little more stuffing in the top part if necessary.

Put two fingers inside the hole at the back and down into the legs, and Walking Trumper is ready to use.

Mr Fingle and Family
(See Airfix Craft Kit, Series 5)

Mr Fingle

You will need

fur fabric, 25cm × 13cm
small quantities of felt and pink foam
joggle eyes
stuffing
needle, cotton, scissors and glue

What you do

Body
From the fur fabric, cut two circles 7·5cm across, and one strip 24cm × 2·5cm.

From the foam, cut one strip 13cm × 10·5cm, and two hands.

ACTUAL SIZE HAND

Sew one edge of the fur strip to a fur circle (furry sides together).

Stitch the other edge to the other circle, leaving about 4cm open.

Turn the right way out.

Stuff, and complete sewing up.

Cut out a mouth and a nose ⌣ ○ and glue them into place.

Glue the joggle eyes in place.

Glue the long foam strip to the underside of the head, making two loops for your fingers.

Glue the hands in place on the outside of the head.

Hat

From the felt, cut two circles – one 5cm across and one 2·5cm across.

Also cut a strip 10cm × 2cm.

Glue the short sides of the strip together to make a tube.

Glue the large circle to one side of the tube and the small one to the other, to make a hat.

Cut out a hat band and glue it round the hat.

Glue the hat to Mr Fingle's head.

Boots

From the felt, cut two pieces 5cm × 2cm and two ovals for the soles.

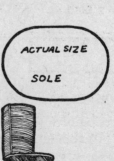

ACTUAL SIZE

SOLE

Glue the shortest sides of the strips together, to make a tube for your fingers.

Glue a sole onto each.

Now Mr Fingle is ready – put your fingers through the foam loops and place the boots on them.

Mrs Fingle

You will need
two different coloured pieces of fur fabric, 25cm × 13cm
small quantities of felt, foam, ribbon and material
joggle eyes and stuffing
needle, cotton, scissors and glue

What you do
Body
Follow the instructions as for Mr Fingle on pages 45 and
46, only cut one of the fur circles from a lighter coloured
fur.

Hat
From the felt, cut two circles 5cm across.

Using long stitches, sew round
the outside of one. Pull the
thread so the edge is gathered.

Glue it to the top of the flat circle.

Decorate with ribbon, sequins etc, from your *bitbox*.

Glue it onto Mrs Fingle's head.

Skirt
Cut a strip of material
15cm × 2.5cm.

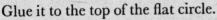

Sew along one edge with long stitches. Pull the thread and
gather it to fit round the top of the foam loops.

Glue or sew the skirt into place.

Boots
Follow the instructions for Mr
Fingle's boots on page 46.

Footballer Fingle

You will need
the same materials as for Mr Fingle
a felt-tip pen

What you do
Follow the instructions as for Mr Fingle,
except for the hat.

Footballer Fingle's hat
From the felt, cut out a circle 13cm across.

Either draw or glue different coloured circles onto the circle.

Gather the outside and pull the thread to fit his head.
Glue it into place.

Scarf
From the felt, cut two strips 5cm × 1·5cm.
Cut one end of each to make a fringe.

Draw or glue on strips of a
different colour.

Glue the scarf into position.

Boots
As for Mr Fingle,
but glue or draw
stripes on them.

Father Christmas Fingle

You will need

red and white fur fabric
red material (for the trousers and hat)
black felt and oddments of pink or red felt
joggle eyes
a small amount of pink foam
stuffing
needle, cotton, scissors and glue

What you do

Body

Follow the instructions as for Mr Fingle on page 45, but cut one red circle and one white circle and one red strip.

To make a white beard, cut a half-circle 5cm across from the fur fabric, and stick it below the mouth.

Hat

Cut a triangle shape from the material, as shown.

Glue the sloping edges together.

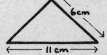

Cut a strip of white fur fabric 11cm × 1cm and glue it round the bottom of the hat.
Glue a small piece of white fur to the point of the hat.

Trousers

From the red material, cut two pieces 5cm × 6cm.

Take one piece of the material and glue half the shorter sides together.

Do the same for the other piece.

Boots

Follow the instructions as for Mr Fingle's boots – but use black felt.

To complete

Glue the open end of the trousers round the foam strip on the bottom of the body, so that you can put your fingers through from the back.

Glue the boots to the other end of the trousers.

8 Finger puppets

**Mouse, Donkey, Owl, Butterfly, Dimble,
Safety Sue, Ebenezer, The Finger Family,
Handy People, Nos 3 and 4 Finger Street**

To help you make the puppets in this chapter, your *bitbox* should have the following things in it:
foam, fur fabric, wool, shirring elastic, felt, paper, rubber bands, egg cartons, sequins, thimble, needle and cotton, shoe box, scissors, felt-tip pens and glue, tracing paper and pencil.

Mouse

You will need
foam or felt
oddments of wool, felt and paper
scissors
glue
pencil and tracing paper

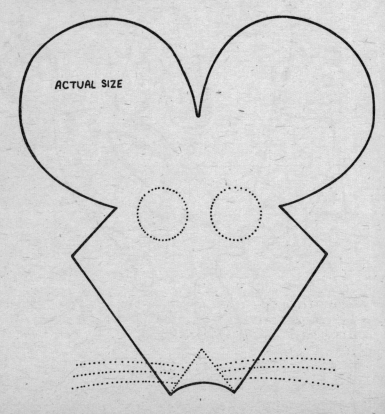

ACTUAL SIZE

What you do

Trace the mouse shape onto the tracing paper, and cut out.

Cut the shape out of foam or felt.

Cut out two eyes from the felt or paper and a triangle nose.

Cut some strands of wool for the whiskers.

Glue the eyes, nose and whiskers into place.

Glue the two straight sides of the shape together.

Donkey

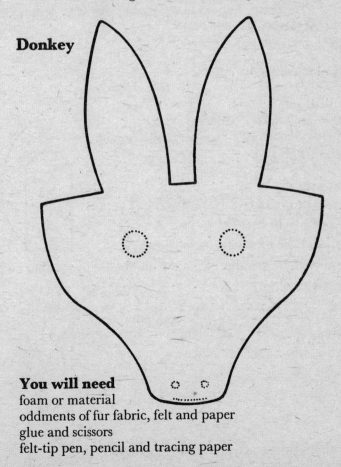

You will need

foam or material
oddments of fur fabric, felt and paper
glue and scissors
felt-tip pen, pencil and tracing paper

What you do

Trace the donkey shape onto the tracing paper, and cut out.

Cut out the shape from the felt or foam.

Cut out two eyes from the felt or paper

and a fur fabric mane.

Glue them into place, as shown.

Using a felt-tip pen, draw on a nose and a mouth.

Spread glue along the two side edges of the head and press them together.

Owl

You will need

felt of several different colours
oddments of material and paper for decoration
scissors and glue

What you do

Cut two pieces of felt the same length as your finger and 1cm wider.

Cut round the top edge, as shown.

Glue the edges together, to make an open-ended tube.

Choose a different colour felt and cut out two large eyes

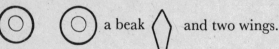

a beak and two wings.

Glue them into place on the finger shape.

Owl is now ready to use.

Butterfly

You will need

felt (a bright colour)   glue and scissors
sequins   pencil and tracing paper

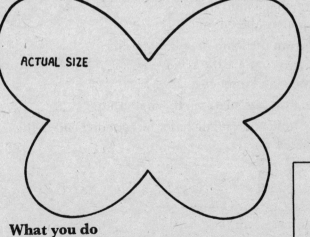

ACTUAL SIZE

What you do

Trace the butterfly shape onto the
tracing paper, and cut out.

Cut out the butterfly shape from the felt.

Cut out a piece of felt 4cm × 2·5cm.

Glue the short sides together to make a tube for your finger.

Decorate the wings with sequins.

Glue the tube to the centre of the underside of the wings.

Put it on your finger and make your butterfly flutter by!

Dimble

You will need
foam or stiff material
thimble
oddments of felt
glue and scissors
tracing paper and pencil

What you do
Trace the shape onto the tracing paper, and cut out.

Cut out from the foam or stiff material.

Cut out two eyes
a small nose and a tongue.

Glue the eyes into place on the foam shape.

Glue the nose and tongue onto the rounded end of the thimble.

Slide the shape onto your finger
and put on the thimble.
Say 'hello' to Dimble!

Safety Sue

You will need
a small ball of 4-ply wool
oddments of wool (pink for the head and another colour for the
   hair)
a pair of No 12 knitting needles

What you do
For the basic body shape (make two pieces alike)
Body: Cast on 10 stitches and knit 16 rows.
Row 17 cast on 4 stitches, knit into the back of the stitches
      then knit to the end of the row.
Row 18 As for Row 17.
Row 19 Cast off 4 stitches then knit to the end of the row.
Row 20 As for Row 19. (10 stitches remain.)
Row 21 Knit 3, knit 2 together, knit 2 together, knit 3.
Row 22 Knit 8.
Row 23 Cast off 1, knit until 2 remain, knit 2 together.
Row 24 Knit 6.
Row 25 **Head:** Change to the pink wool and continue
      knitting, increasing 1 stitch at the beginning of
      the next 4 rows.
Row 30 (10 stitches.) Knit 4 rows.
Row 35 Decrease 1 stitch at the beginning of the next 4
      rows.
Row 39 Cast off 6 stitches.

Sew the two basic body shapes together.

Embroider eyes, a nose and a mouth on one side of the
head to make a face.

Cut some wool into strands, plait it for hair and fix in
place.

For the hat Cast on 20 stitches and knit 12 rows. Cast off.

Fold the strip in half and sew it together down one side.

Sew the hat onto Sue's head.

Now turn to the 'Safety Sue Story' on page 89.

Ebenezer

You will need

a pink cardboard egg carton (the sort with long pointed parts
  separating the eggs)
some scruffy long fur fabric or wool
glue, scissors and felt-tip pen

What you do

From the bottom section of the carton cut two egg sections
and one separator (this will make the eyes and nose).

On the inside of the egg sections draw two black circles for
eyes.

For Ebenezer's chin, cut a half-circle 8cm across from the
lid of the egg carton. Slice a piece out, as shown.

Glue it into place underneath the nose.

Glue fur all round for hair and a beard.

Hat

Cut another egg section from the egg carton.

Cut one half of it away, so that
the remaining piece can
be bent to form a peak.

Glue it into place on top of the head.

Insert two fingers in the back of his nose to make him
move.

The Finger Family

You will need
the fingers of one hand
a felt-tip pen

What you do
With the felt-tip pen draw the Finger Family.

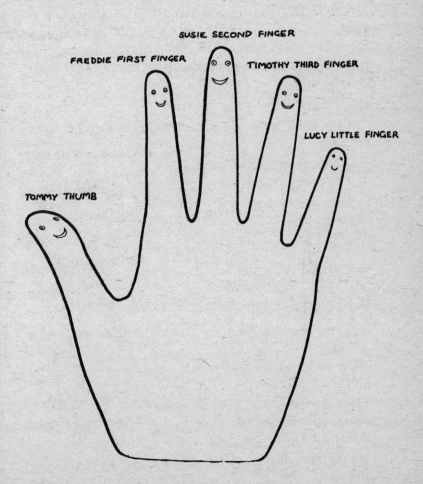

Handy People

You will need (to make two)
1 pair of hands
2 small pieces of material (or crêpe paper) 15cm × 18cm
oddments of wool
shirring elastic
2 rubber bands
felt-tip pen

What you do

Skirt
Stitch the elastic through the long edge of the material or paper. (Measure it to fit round your knuckles.) Tie the ends together.

Hair
Cut several lengths of wool and tie them together at the centre.

Tie this onto a rubber band which will fit round your wrist.

Draw a face on the back of your hand.

Draw shoes on the first and second fingers.

Place the rubber band (with hair) round your wrist and the skirt round your knuckles.

Do the same for the other hand and you have two 'Handy People'.

Handy People's Houses

To make No 3 and No 4 Finger Street you will need

1 shoe box
felt-tip pens
oddments of paper
glue and scissors

What you do

Draw a line round three sides of the box, 2cm from the bottom.

Cut along it and remove the three sides.

Cut a piece 2cm wide from one of the short sides you have just cut off.

Place this down the middle of
the bottom of the box to
make two parts (gardens).

Make a gate for each garden by cutting through the 'fence' and along the bottom. It can then be bent to make the gate open and shut.

Draw and cut out two paper houses and glue them onto the inside of the tall side of the box.

From the lid of the shoe box,
cut two pieces the same size
as the gardens.

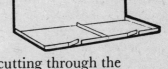

On one draw and colour in
flowers, and on the other
vegetables.

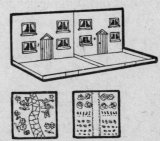

Now make up a story for your
Handy People and act it
out in your 'theatre'.

9 Fur fabric and material puppets

Pickle, Fluffy Woppit, Panda

Most of the things used in this chapter need to be bought, although your *bitbox* will still be a great help to you if it has the following things in it:
oddments of felt and material, tracing paper and pencil, needle, cotton, scissors and glue.

Pickle

You will need
shaggy fur fabric, about 45cm × 45cm
oddments of felt
large joggle eyes
needle, cotton, scissors and glue

What you do
Cut out two pieces of fur fabric to fit your arm, each one about 15cm × 30 cm.

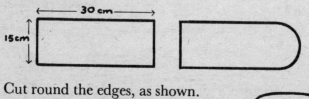

Cut round the edges, as shown.

Cut an oval of pink felt exactly
the same size as these ends.

With the right sides of the material together – insert the felt oval, folded in half.

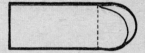

Sew half of the felt oval to the top piece of foam and the other half to the bottom piece, to make a mouth.

Sew the rest of the fur fabric together, leaving the short straight edges open.

Turn the right way out and push the pink felt inside to make a mouth.

Glue the eyes into place. (If you don't have any joggle eyes, you could make some from felt.)

Cut out a nose ⃝ two ears and a tongue from the felt and glue them in place.

Tail

Cut a piece of fur fabric – 24cm × 4cm, with a point at one end, as shown.

4 cm

← 24 cm →

Sew or glue the long sides together and attach the tail to the top of the body.

Put your arm inside.
Place your fingers inside the top of the mouth and your thumb in the bottom part.
Open and close to make Pickle talk.

Fluffy Woppit

You will need

shaggy long fur fabric, about 40cm × 18cm
joggle eyes
oddments of felt
1 piece of material 15cm × 45cm
scissors, needle, cotton and glue
tracing paper and pencil

What you do

Trace the Woppit shape onto the
tracing paper, and cut out.

Put the paper shape on the
fur fabric and cut two.

With the right sides together,
sew round the fur shape,
leaving the straight bottom edge open.

To make the skirt
Take the piece of material 15cm × 45cm. With the right
sides inside, sew or glue the short sides together.

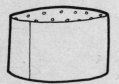

Hem the bottom edge of the skirt.

Gather the top edge to fit the
straight edge of the fur shape.
Turn both the fur shape and
the skirt the right way out.

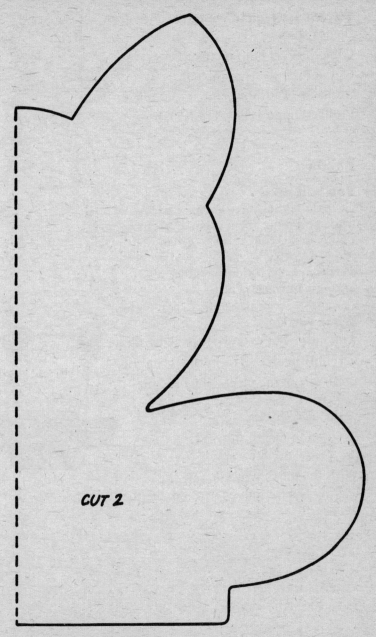

CUT 2

PLACE ON FOLD

Sew the skirt to the bottom of the fur shape.

Glue the eyes onto the face.

Cut out a nose from the felt (or use a bead) and glue it into place.

Fluffy Woppit is now ready to use.

Panda

You will need

black fur fabric, about 23cm × 23cm
white fur fabric, about 20cm × 10cm
1 piece of material 13cm × 38 cm (for the skirt)
oddments of felt
scissors, needle, cotton and glue
tracing paper and pencil

What you do

Trace the shapes onto the tracing paper.

Cut out the shapes from the fur fabric.

Onto one of the pieces of white fur, sew two ears and one of the arm shapes.

Do the same with the other piece of white fur.

With the fur side inside, sew the two shapes together, leaving the bottom edge of the head and Panda's 'waist' open.

The skirt
With the right sides inside, join the two short sides of the material together.
Turn the right way out.

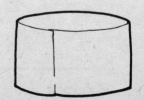

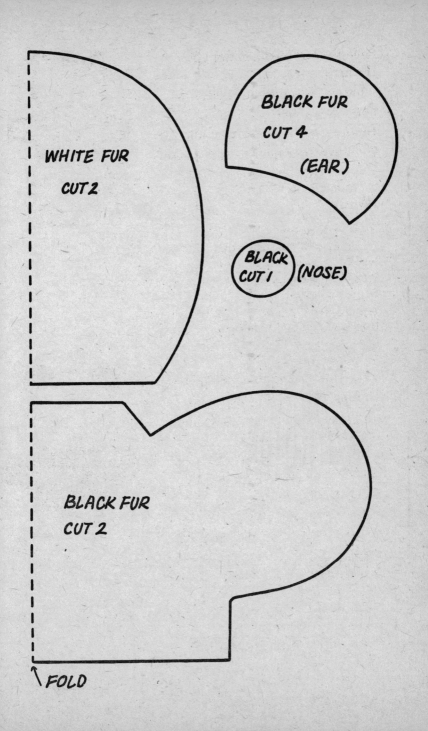

Hem the bottom edge of the skirt.

Gather the top edge and fit it to the bottom edge of the fur shape.

Sew the two together.

Cut out two black felt eyes and glue them into place.

Cut two small white circles and glue one in the centre of each black circle.

Glue the black furry nose in place.

10 Puppets that are harder to make

Softy Rag Doll Puppet, Tinkle, Cushion Puppet, Daffodil, Pop-up Clowns, Pop-up Policeman and Lollipop Man

Some of the things in this chapter need to be bought but your *bitbox* will be a great help to you, especially if it has the following things in it:

oddments of felt, foam, wool, lace, fur fabric, shirring elastic, sequins, cardboard, yoghurt cartons, cornflakes box, wallpaper, scissors, needle, cotton and glue, felt-tip pens, pencil and tracing paper.

Softy Rag Doll Puppet

You will need
pink material – 2 squares 20cm × 20cm
print material – 3 squares 18cm × 18cm
pink foam – 2 strips 18cm × 2·5cm × 0·5cm
shirring elastic
oddments of felt, wool and lace
scissors, needle, cotton and glue
pencil and paper

What you do
Lay your hand on a piece of paper, fingers spread, and draw round it – making your thumb and little finger into 'arms'.

Cut out the hand shape and pin it to the two squares of pink material. Cut it out.

Sew the two pieces together, with the right sides inside, and leave the straight edge open.

Turn the right way out.

Cut out two felt eyes ◯ ◯
a nose ◯
a mouth ‿
and two hands. ◯ ◯

Glue them in place

Cut some wool into strands about 45cm long for hair.
Glue or sew it round the face and make two plaits.

Cut eight small pieces of wool and glue
them round the eyes to make eyelashes.

Legs
Cut out a pair of shoes from felt.
Cut four pieces, as shown.

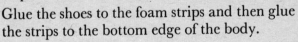

← 2.5cm →

Glue two pieces together
round the curved edges.
Repeat for the other shoe.

Glue the shoes to the foam strips and then glue
the strips to the bottom edge of the body.

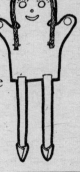

Dress
Put the two squares of print material together
and cut them into a dress shape, as shown.

Sew the sides and shoulders together,
leaving the neck, arms and bottom open.

Hem round the arms, neck and bottom and
decorate with lace.

Mob cap
From the other square of print cut a
circle 13cm across.

Sew lace round the outside of the circle.

Stitch shirring elastic about 2·5cm inside the edge of the circle, as shown.

Gather it to fit her head and tie or sew the ends together.

Sew or stick the hat into place and put on her dress.

Softy Rag Doll Puppet is now ready to use.

Tinkle

You will need

brightly coloured material – 2 squares 20cm × 20cm, 1 piece 15cm × 10cm
a small amount of stuffing
a polystyrene ball 6cm across
2 small bells (from a craft shop)
a small quantity of felt
oddments of felt, fur fabric, sequins, cardboard, etc (*bitbox*)
a large plastic bead (for the nose)
scissors, needle, cotton and glue
tracing paper and pencil

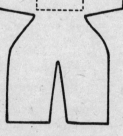

What you do

Body

Trace the pattern onto the tracing paper and pin it onto the two 20cm squares. Cut it out.

With the right sides inside, sew the two body shapes together – leaving the straight ends of the arms and legs and neck open.

Decide which is to be the back and cut out a piece as shown.

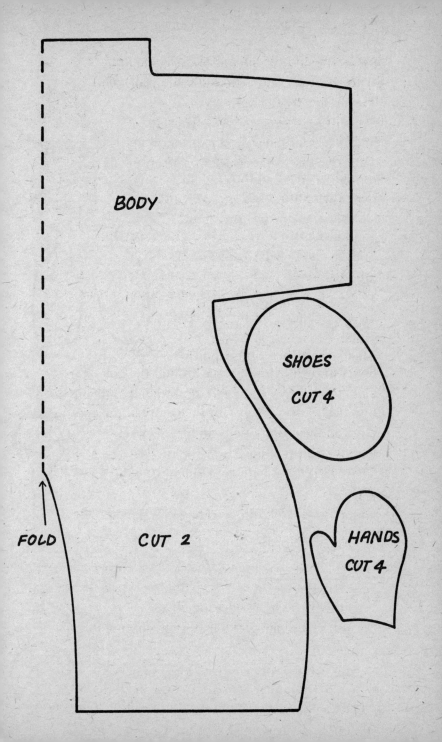

Stitch thread through the open edges of the
arms and legs, pull them tight and fasten off.

Turn the body the right way out.

Trace the patterns and from the felt cut
four pieces for hands and four pieces for feet.

Take two of the hand pieces, glue or sew them
round the edges and stuff slightly.
Glue them into place.

Do the same for the other hand
and for the two feet.

Stuff the body below waist level.

Head
Make a hole in the ball –
big enough for your finger and
about 1cm deep.

Make a cardboard tube to fit your
finger and glue it into place around the hole.

Cut out two eyes and a mouth from felt and glue them
into place – use sequins for the centre of the eyes.

Glue on the red plastic bead for the nose.

Cut out a strip of fur fabric about
21cm × 1cm for hair, and glue it round the face.

Hat
Cut a piece of felt into a triangle, as shown.

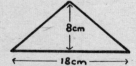

Glue the two shorter sides together.

Decorate with pieces of felt and glue it onto the head.

Ruff
Cut three different coloured circles of felt, one
5cm across, another 6cm across and the third
7cm across. Cut a hole in the middle of each one

and fit them onto the tube, the smallest one first. Sew the two bells onto the ruff.

To complete
Gather the neck of the body and glue it to the bottom of the tube.

Cut a collar from a strip of felt 18cm × 4cm.

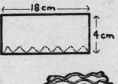

Fit it round the neck to hide the tube, and glue it into place.

If you want to hide your hand while manipulating Tinkle, make a cover by cutting the 15cm × 10cm piece of material into a half-circle. Gather the straight edge with shirring elastic.

Glue the cover into place along its curved edge over the 'hole' in Tinkle's back.

Decorate the body with gaily coloured felt, or sequins, and Tinkle is ready to use.

Cushion puppet – Tortoise

You will need
a circle of fur fabric 38cm across
a circle of material 38cm across
2 pieces of material 38cm × 20cm
a piece of felt 15cm × 11cm
needle, cotton, scissors and glue

oddments of felt
stuffing
joggle eyes
tracing paper and pencil

What you do

Cushion

Enlarge the pattern to the right size on a piece of paper
21cm × 32½cm.*

Cut out the pattern pieces.

With the right sides together, sew round the curved edges
of the feet and tail.

Turn the right way out, and stuff.

Tack the straight edges together.

Place them in position, as shown,
on the circle of material, right side up.

Place the fur circle on top, right side down.
Sew them all together,
leaving a small opening.

Turn it the right way out and stuff.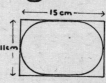
Complete the sewing up.

Head

Cut the pieces of felt into an oval.

With the material right sides together,
insert the felt oval, folded in half.

Sew half of the felt to the
top piece of material,
and the other half to the bottom piece,
to make a mouth.

Sew the rest of the material together,
leaving the straight edge open.

Turn the right way out.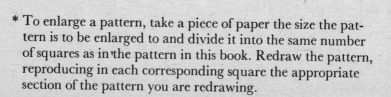

* To enlarge a pattern, take a piece of paper the size the pattern is to be enlarged to and divide it into the same number
  of squares as in the pattern in this book. Redraw the pattern,
  reproducing in each corresponding square the appropriate
  section of the pattern you are redrawing.

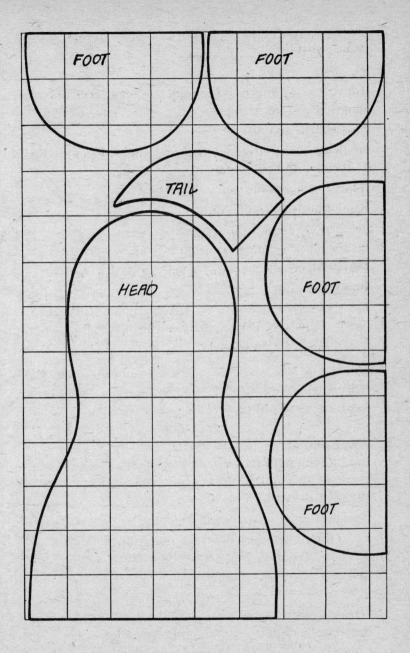

Glue the joggle eyes onto a
slightly larger piece of felt and
glue them into place on the head.

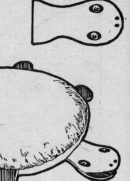

Cut two small circles of felt and
glue them on for the nose.

Glue or sew one side of
the head onto the
underside of the body.

Neaten the edges.

Insert your hand and you
have a cushion puppet to cuddle!

Daffodil

You will need

a sheet of yellow foam,
   approximately 45cm × 45cm
gingham material,
   68cm × 68cm
oddments of foam and felt

needle, cotton, scissors, glue
tracing paper
ribbon and lace
yellow joggle eyes
a small amount of stuffing

Note All foam parts must be glued together with the
correct type of glue.

What you do

Enlarge the pattern to the right size on a piece of paper
55cm × 47.5 cm. To do this follow the instructions in the
footnote on page 76.

Cut out the pattern pieces.

Place the pattern pieces on the materials as follows:
pieces 1, 2, 3, 4, 6, 7 and 8 – yellow foam
pieces 9, 10 and 11 – gingham
piece 5 – pink foam

Cut them out.

Find the head gusset (3) and glue one edge
round the front head (1) and the other edge
round the back head (2).

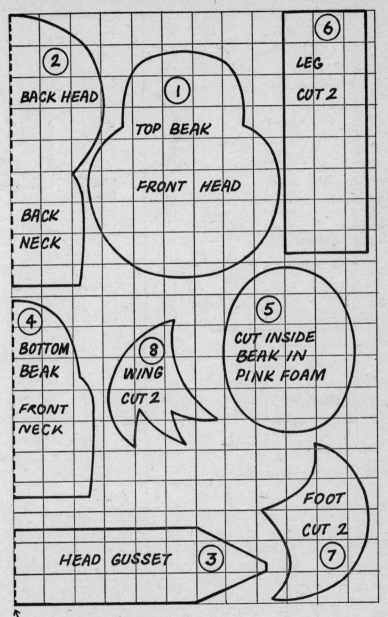

PLACE ON FOLD

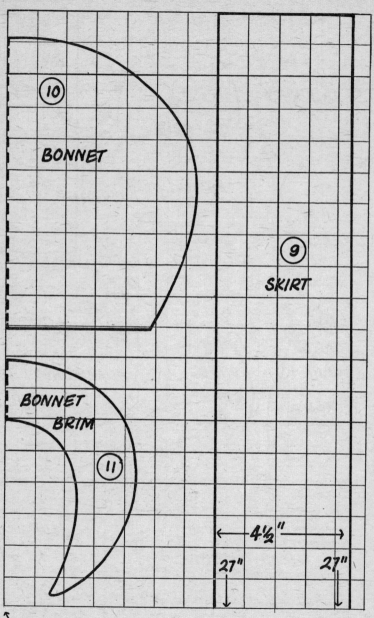

PLACE ON FOLD

Glue the front neck (4) to the back neck (2) at the sides.

Glue the pink part of the beak (5) to the beak parts of 1 and 4 (edges only).

Slightly stuff the head, leaving enough room to insert your hand.

Cut outer eyes of black felt and inner ones of white felt.

Glue them into position with the joggle eyes on top.

Legs

Make pattern piece 6 into a roll and glue it together.

Glue a foot onto one end.

Glue the other end to the bottom of the neck (4).

Do the same with the other leg.

Wings

Glue them in place just below the beak, as shown.

Dress

Select pattern piece 9 and sew the short edges together.

Hem along one side and gather the other.

Fit it round Daffodil's middle – just below her wings – and sew it in place.

Bonnet

With the right sides inside, sew the outer edges of pattern pieces 10 and 11 together.

Turn the right way out and gather the other edges to fit the head.

Sew on ribbon ties and decorate with lace.

Glue the bonnet onto Daffodil's head, and she is ready to use.

Pop-up Clowns

You will need

5 pieces of material 25cm × 20cm,
    each with a different pattern
5 yoghurt cartons
5 pieces of dowel, each about 25cm long
    (obtainable from any 'Do-it-yourself' shop)
5 ping-pong or polystyrene balls
a large empty cornflakes box (or any box of a similar size)
old pieces of wallpaper
oddments of wool, felt, cardboard, sequins etc (*bitbox*)
glue, felt-tip pens and scissors

What you do

To make one clown:

Draw or glue features and hair onto a ball.

Make a hole in the neck part and glue it onto one end of a piece of dowel.

Glue the longest sides of one of the pieces of material together.

Stitch one end and gather it to fit the clown's neck.

Glue it into position.

Make a hole in the bottom of a yoghurt carton to fit the dowel.

Put the dowel through from the inside of the carton and guide the material over the outside.

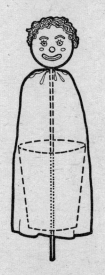 

Glue the bottom edge of the material to the bottom of the carton.

Make a hat – either a triangle or a circle or a moulded milk top etc.

Make four more clowns in the same way.

Box

Cut out either the back or the front of
the box and cover
the rest with wallpaper.

Stand the box on one of its long sides.

Make five holes in the top.

Guide the rods through and glue the bottom of the
cartons to the top of the box.

See how to use your Pop-up
Clowns on page 95.

Pop-up Policeman and Lollipop Man

You will need

a shoe box (without the lid)
2 yoghurt cartons
2 pieces of dowel, each approximately 25cm long
2 ping-pong or polystyrene balls
white paper (to cover the box)
a piece of white material 25cm × 20cm
a piece of dark blue material 25cm × 20cm
oddments of pink felt, foil, fur fabric etc (*bitbox*)
papier mâché* for the helmet and Lollipop Man's hat
paint and plasticine
scissors, felt-tip pens and glue

What you do

Follow the basic instructions for making the Pop-up
Clown on page 83.

* How to make papier mâché: Tear up some newspaper into
very small pieces and soak them in water. Mix up the paper
until it looks smooth and greyish. Squeeze off the extra water.
Now add a little cold-water paste (used for hanging
wallpaper) – two parts of pulp to one part paste. Make a
mould from plasticine and cover the top with the papier
mâché. Leave it to dry, then take out the plasticine mould,
and paint.

To make the shoulders and arms

Take the material and fold it in half along the longer side.

Glue or sew it along the side and top edges, leaving a small hole for the neck.

Turn the right way out.

Cut out hands from the pink felt and stick them in place.

For the Lollipop Man

Use white material and mould a hat for him from papier mâché.

Make him a sign from cardboard
and attach it to
his right arm, as shown.

Draw on his buttons with
a felt-tip pen.

For the Policeman

Use dark material and
mould his helmet from
papier mâché.

Make his buttons and
badge from silver foil.

To make the box

If not already plain, cover it with white paper.

Draw a simple road with a pavement and
Zebra Crossing on the bottom of the box.

Make two holes in the top edge and
guide the rods through.

Glue the bottoms of the cartons to
the top of the box.

See how to use on page 86.

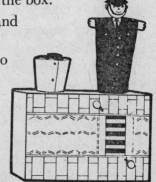

11 For parents, teachers and playgroup people

Puppets with a purpose, Other uses for puppets, Lap-theatre, Stories, Pop-up Clowns' Rhyme

Puppets with a purpose

Communication is probably the most important aspect of working with puppets. Yet it happens almost as an extra and without anyone really trying. Whether you are working with one child or with a group, the communication starts with finding the materials and continues as you work together making the puppets.

Puppets are **fun**, and learning with them is fun. From an early age children are used to being entertained by television, which means that for them the written word is often boring. Puppets are an intermediate stage – one step away from television and one step into books.

Counting Numbers can be taught with the aid of the Pop-up Clowns (page 82) and their rhyme on page 95. These can also be used to illustrate any other counting rhymes.

Colours Mr Round (page 13) and the Trumper Cut-out (page 24) will help children to recognize colours.

Safety The Pop-up Policeman and Lollipop Man on page 84 have been approved by Road Safety Officers as being a particularly effective way of introducing ways of crossing the road – remembering of course that *no pre-school* child is capable of crossing alone.

The Mitten Trumper (page 40) helps children to be seen, as well as being waterproof.

Safety Sue (page 57) and her special story on page 89 is written for indoor safety.

Relaxation, when ill at home or in hospital – Mickey Hankey and Sally Spoon.

Observation The Happy/Sad Puppet (page 14) can be used to 'spot the differences'.

Milly Mop (page 22) – observe the everyday things she is made from.

Fun!

By the time you reach this part you will have realized that using puppets is fun – so this aspect of working with puppets needs no explanation!

Other uses for puppets

Many traditional rhymes and stories can be illustrated with the puppets in this book.

Here are a few suggestions:

Humpty Dumpty	Mr Fingle and Mr Round
Little Miss Muffet	Any one of the mop and spoon puppets. Softy Rag Doll and Spider
Jack and Jill	Tish and Ooo or the Happy/Sad puppet
Little Boy Blue	Bluey
Hickory Dickory Dock	Mouse Finger Puppet
Pussy cat, pussy cat and *I love little pussy*	Pickle or Kitten Mitten
Old Mother Hubbard	Polly and Dimble
Grand Old Duke of York	any of the 'walking puppets', for example Walking Trumper, Mr Fingle and Mr Round

Incy Wincy Spider	Spider
Little Red Riding Hood	Polly or any other girl puppet. Fluffy Woppit could be the wolf.
Cinderella	Softy Rag Doll (Cinderella), Funny Face and Frog (Ugly Sisters), Tinkle or Matchbox Clown (Buttons), Trumper or Mr Fingle (Prince)
Dick Whittington	Mr Round or Mr Fingle (Dick), Pickle or Kitten Mitten (cat)

I'm sure that now you have started there are lots of other stories and rhymes you can think of. Of course, you can always make up your own too!

Lap-theatre

Note This theatre is designed to fit on your lap, but it is just as effective on a table top. With the outside facing the audience, you can hide your hands, props and puppets inside.

Most of the puppets in this book are shown to their best advantage using this prop. Remember – whenever you are using more than one puppet, *move only the one that is talking*.

It is a good idea to practise in front of a mirror.

You will need
a cardboard box about 40cm long, 28cm high and at least 15cm wide
odd pieces of wallpaper (a brick or stone design if possible)
pictures of trees and flowers which you can cut out
glue and scissors

What you do
Keeping one side of the box as it is, cut the rest into the following shape.

Left as it is,
it can be folded flat.

If you want to secure it,
join the bottom to
the sides.

To decorate
Cover with wallpaper.
Either use cut-outs from
old magazines or
make your own
trees and flowers.

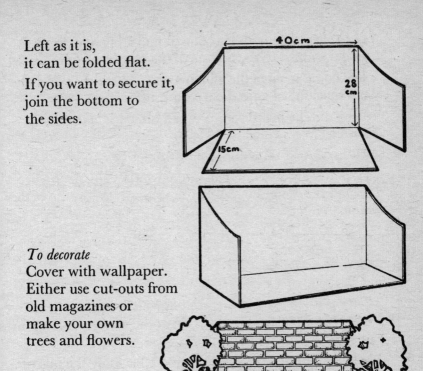

Safety Sue Story

(Safety Sue puppet – page 57)

Patsy and Peter are twins and although they are alike in
many ways, there is one big difference. Patsy is usually
good and Peter is usually naughty. It seemed to Patsy as if
she were always rescuing her brother. She wished she
could find a way to cure him.

Today it is raining and they have to stay inside. Big
raindrops are falling onto the window pane.

'I bet I can find a bigger raindrop than you can,' said
Peter.

They spent a long time trying to find a big one. Every time it slipped to the bottom of the pane and disappeared.

'I'm going to open the window and catch one,' said Peter and he climbed onto the window sill.

As he did, he heard someone call his name. He knew it wasn't Patsy's voice.

'Did you hear something?' he asked as he climbed down.

Then he saw a movement on the window sill, near where he had been standing. A tiny person was there – no bigger than a finger.

'How do you do?
    I'm Safety Sue.
Please remember what I say,
    Be very careful every day.'

Peter just looked and Sue continued in a squeaky voice. 'It's very dangerous to stand up in the window and try to open it.'

Peter still didn't say anything and once more the tiny voice said –

'How do you do?
    I'm Safety Sue.
Please remember what I say,
    Be very careful every day,'

and she disappeared.

'Where's she gone?' said Peter. He looked all around the room and even behind the curtains, but he couldn't see her.

'I'm going to tell Mum about her,' he said.

Patsy followed him into the kitchen but their Mother wasn't there.

'I expect she's upstairs,' said Patsy. 'Come on, we're not supposed to stay in here unless someone is with us.'

Peter seemed to have forgotten all about Safety Sue, he was interested in looking at the kitchen – particularly the cooker.

'I wonder what's for dinner?' he said, and moved towards the cooker – an extremely hot cooker, with pots of boiling water on the top.

'Peter – please come on,' pleaded Patsy.

He pretended not to hear. He had almost reached the cooker when he heard the squeaky voice again. He stopped and turned his head – there sitting on his shoulder was Safety Sue.

'How do you do?
   I'm Safety Sue.
Please remember what I say,
   Be very careful every day.'

'Where did you come from?' he asked. 'I looked everywhere for you just now.'

'That's a secret,' she said. 'But this time I've come to tell you about hot cookers. Surely you know you must never go near them – particularly when there are hot pans on the top.'

'Well, yes – I know. I thought it would be fun to peep inside a pan – I'm sorry.'

'You are an extremely silly boy,' Sue replied. 'You should try to be more like Patsy.'

Peter didn't like that very much and whilst he was thinking how to reply Sue said –

How do you do?
   I'm Safety Sue.
Please remember what I say,
   Be very careful, every day,'

and she disappeared again.

Patsy laughed. 'You do look silly.'

'I'm not silly,' he replied. 'And I don't like you laughing at me.'

'I was laughing at Safety Sue,' said Patsy. 'I'm happy you listen to what she tells you.'

'Well, she's so tiny and knows so much.'

When Patsy heard him say that, she put her hand in her pocket and brought out Safety Sue and said in a tiny squeaky voice –

'How do you do?
 I'm Safety Sue.
Please remember what I say,
 Be very careful every day.'

'It was *you* all the time!' Peter cried.

'Yes,' said Patsy. 'Mummy helped me to make her and Safety Sue always reminds me to be careful. I expect Mummy will make one for you too.'

The twins found their mother and she did make one for Peter. Now they are more alike than ever – because they both have a Safety Sue.

Octopus and the Little Fishes

Note This is a story illustrated with puppets. You will need one person to read the story and do all the voices, and one to manipulate the puppets and do all the actions.

What you need

Octopus   page 27
Fishes   page 25
Lap theatre page 88 (made into an undersea scene)
A large pebble (for the rock)

(*Octopus is sitting on a rock, asleep*)

Under the sea lives an octopus – a rather grumpy octopus.

(*Octopus moves and snores*)

The reason he is grumpy is because no one will play with him.

The fish are frightened he will eat them, so they keep out of his way.

(*Octopus moves and snores again*)

I am going to tell you the story of what happened one day when Octopus was asleep – just like he is now.

(*Octopus snores*)

Several little fish wanted the rock to play hide-and-seek behind.

(*fish appear*)

They swam round and round and looked at Octopus – but made sure they didn't get too close.

'We shall have to find another rock,' said one called Splish.

'No, I want to play here,' said Splash.

'Shh – we will wake him if we make too much noise.'

(*Octopus moves and snores*)

'I don't care – I'm not afraid of him,' said Splash.

'He might eat us,' replied Splish.

'No, he won't – Octopuses don't eat fish.'

(*they swim nearer to Octopus and he moves and wakes up. Fish back away.*)

'I thought you said you were not frightened. Why did you swim away?' asked Splish.

'I didn't swim away – he just made me jump,' answered Splash.

Octopus heard the fish arguing and asked, 'What's all this noise about?'

'We were only swimming around,' they answered.

'Come closer – let me have a look at you.'

The fish didn't really want to go any closer, in case he was angry.

'Come on, come on, hurry up,' said Octopus.

Slowly they swam towards him, gradually getting closer. Then one pushed another right against Octopus's legs.

They all jumped back and when they looked, were surprised to see Octopus rolling about laughing.

(*Octopus jumping up and down*)

'Ha-ha-ha!' he laughed. 'You tickled my toes – do it again.'

The fish swam back towards him and cautiously tickled his toes.

(*the fish jump back again when Octopus laughs*)

'Ha-ha-ha! I had forgotten how good it is to laugh.'

The fish realized then that the Octopus was friendly and wanted to play with them. So they tickled him again.

They played the game until they were tired, and then they remembered the reason they were there.

'You're sitting on our rock,' said Splash. 'It's the one we use to play hide-and-seek.'

'Oh dear, I'm very sorry,' replied Octopus. 'I'll jump off and find another one. Although it is very comfortable – it's so round and smooth.'

The little fishes talked to one another and decided that as the Octopus had been so friendly, they would let him stay there.

'That's alright,' said Splash. 'We'll find another rock. If you stay there we shall know where to find you tomorrow.'

'What a good idea,' said Octopus. 'See you tomorrow then,' and he fell asleep again.

(*Octopus snores*)

'I told you he wouldn't eat us,' said Splash. 'I like our new friend,' and they all swam away and left Octopus to have a rest.

(*fish swim away*)

Pop-up Clowns' Rhyme

(Pop-up Clowns – page 83)

With the clowns all inside their pots and the front of the box facing your audience, bring them slowly out – counting as you do so:

1 – 2 – 3 – 4 – 5
Five funny clowns – would like to find some more.
One went to look for some – (*pop him down*)
then there were *four*!

Four funny clowns – climbed into a tree.
One got stuck up there – (*pop him down*)
then there were *three*!

Three funny clowns – didn't know what to do.
One went on holiday – (*pop him down*)
then there were *two*!

Two funny clowns – sitting in the sun.
One fell fast asleep – (*pop him down*)
then there was *one*!

One funny clown – cried and cried all day.
They put him in a motor car – (*pop him down*)
and sent him miles away!

Elizabeth Gundrey
Make Your Own Monster 25p

Simple instructions for making monsters of all kinds – from dressing up as a ghost to making a dragon mask, a bat mobile or an abominable snowman.

Collecting Things 30p

Exciting and practical ideas on how to start over one hundred collections ; none of them is expensive and none takes up too much room. There are clear instructions for the best ways of arranging your collection and plenty of useful addresses.

Making Decorations 25p

A simple, instructive and readable handbook on making decorations out of everyday things for Christmas, Easter, birthday parties and Hallowe'en.

Sewing Things 35p

The reader is taken step by step through the first stages of sewing and presented with ideas on things to make. All is clearly and practically explained.

Growing Things 25p

A useful and enthusiastic gardening book for an absolute beginner – with hints on growing attractive plants from everyday fruits and vegetables, and instructions on how to make such things as underwater gardens, hanging baskets and window boxes.

Michael Harvey and Rae Compton
Knitting Things 40p

A simple guide containing all you need to know to start knitting with lots of attractive patterns.